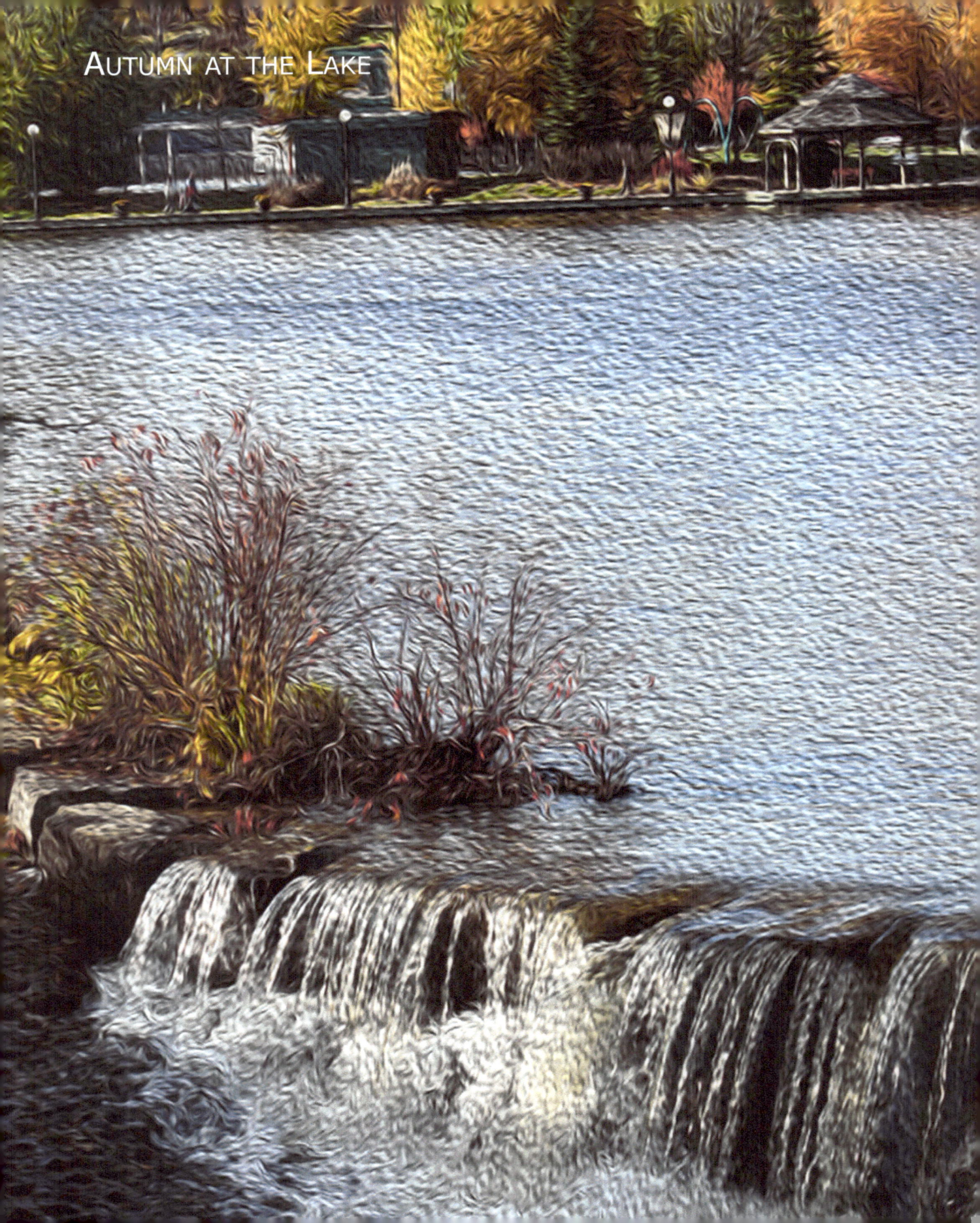

Autumn at the Lake

Art through Photography

ART/PHOTOGRAPHY

KLAUS D. EMRICH

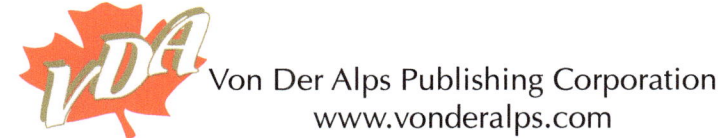
Von Der Alps Publishing Corporation
www.vonderalps.com

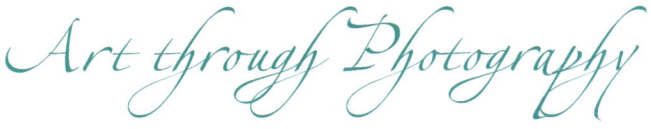

Artist/Author/Photographer

Klaus D. Emrich

First original published in April 2014 by
Von Der Alps Publishing Corporation, CANADA.

www.vonderalps.com

Canadian Cataloguing in Publication Data
ISBN 978-0-9936867-0-2

Printed in USA

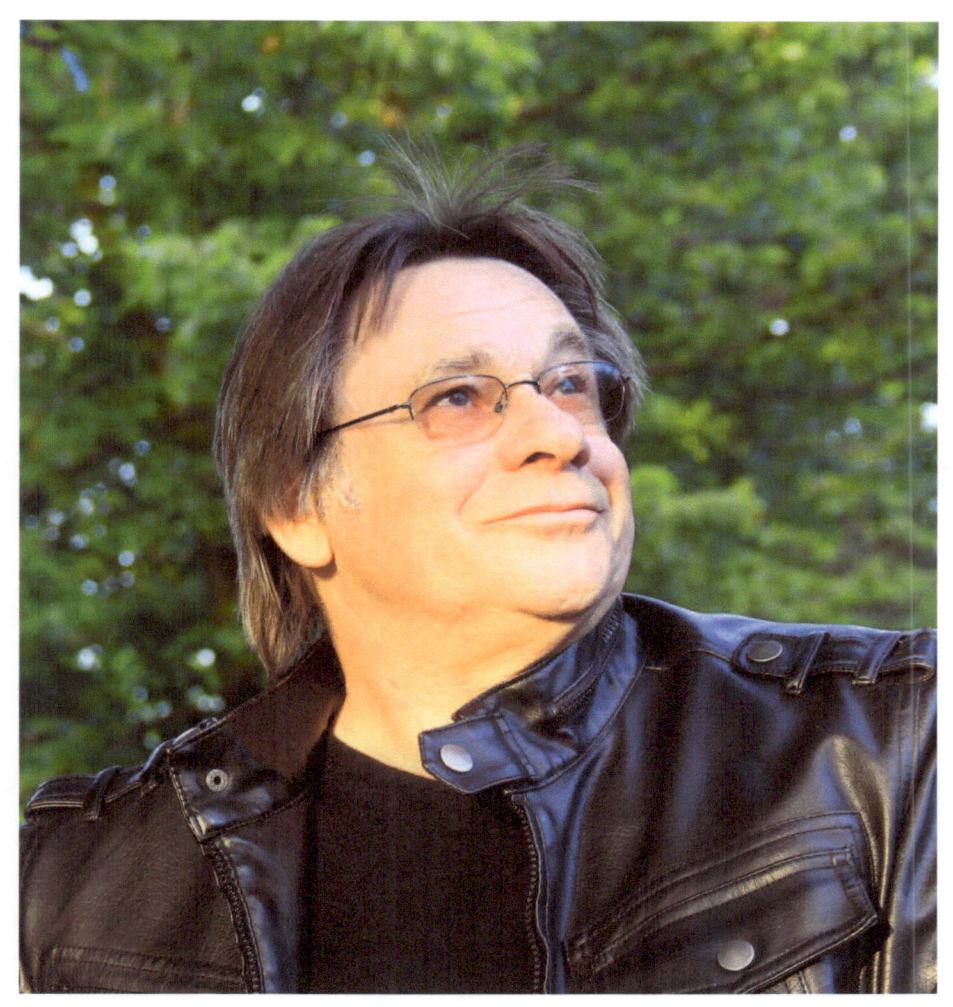

KLAUS D. EMRICH

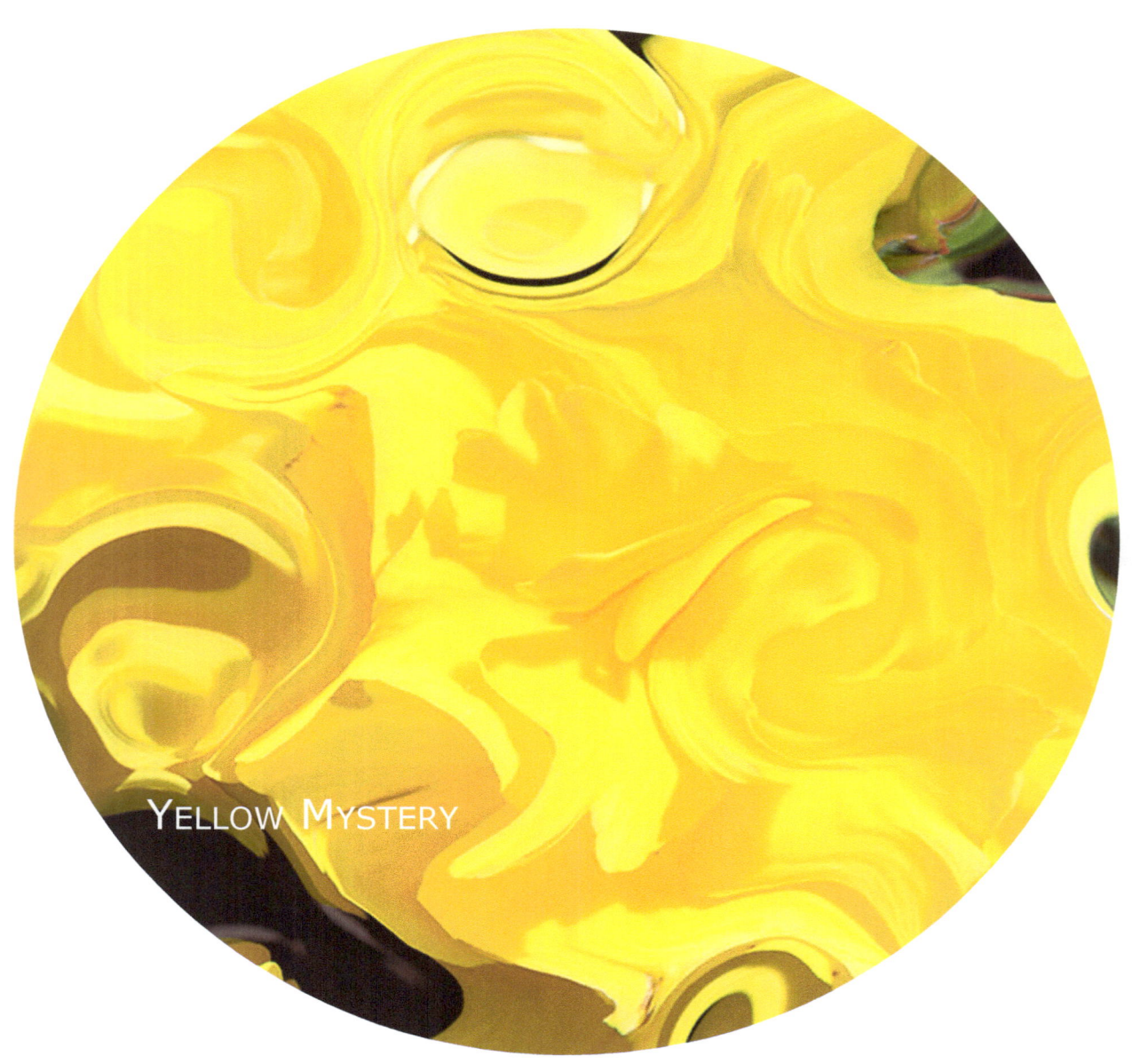

Yellow Mystery

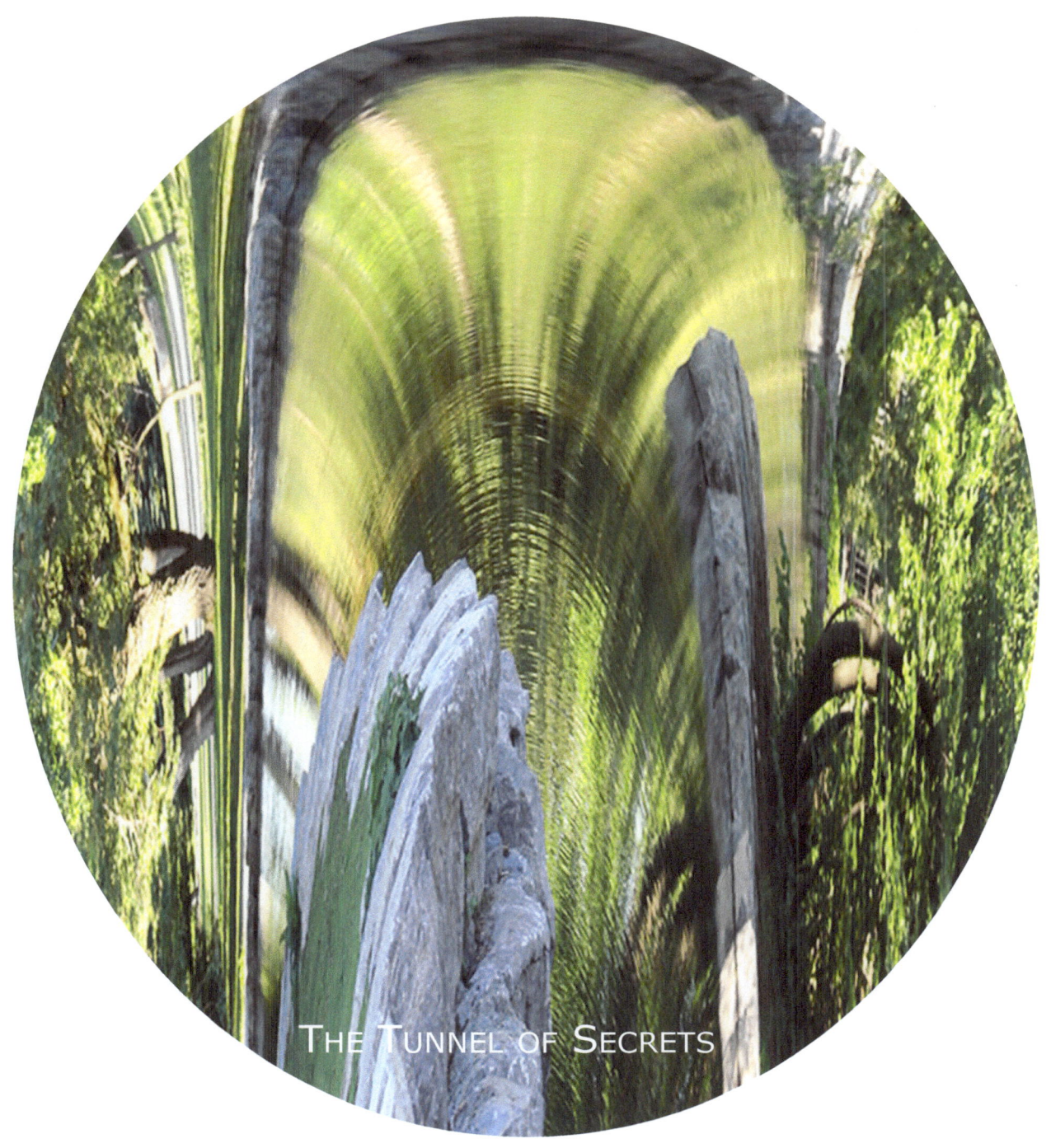

THE TUNNEL OF SECRETS

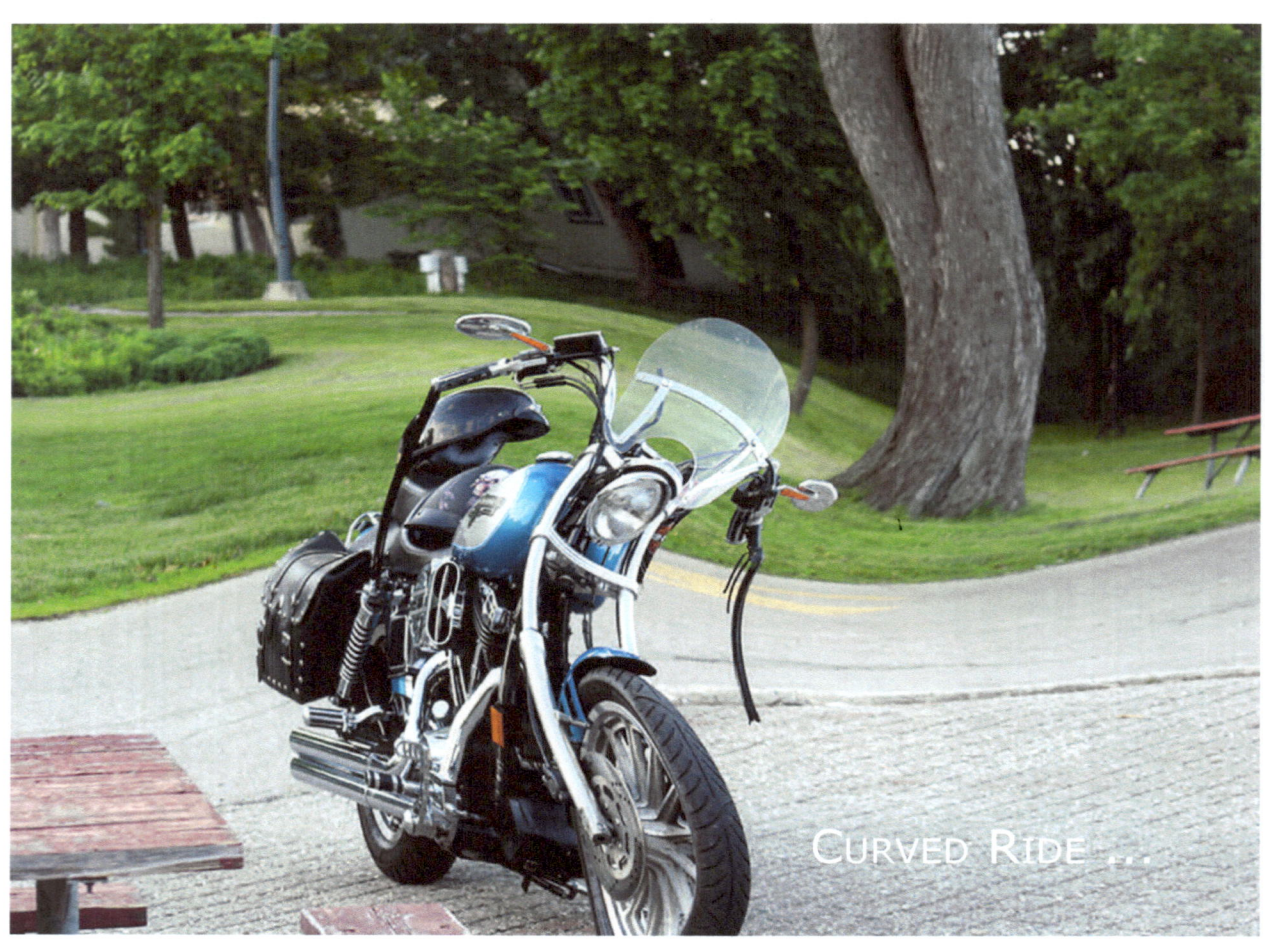

CURVED RIDE ...

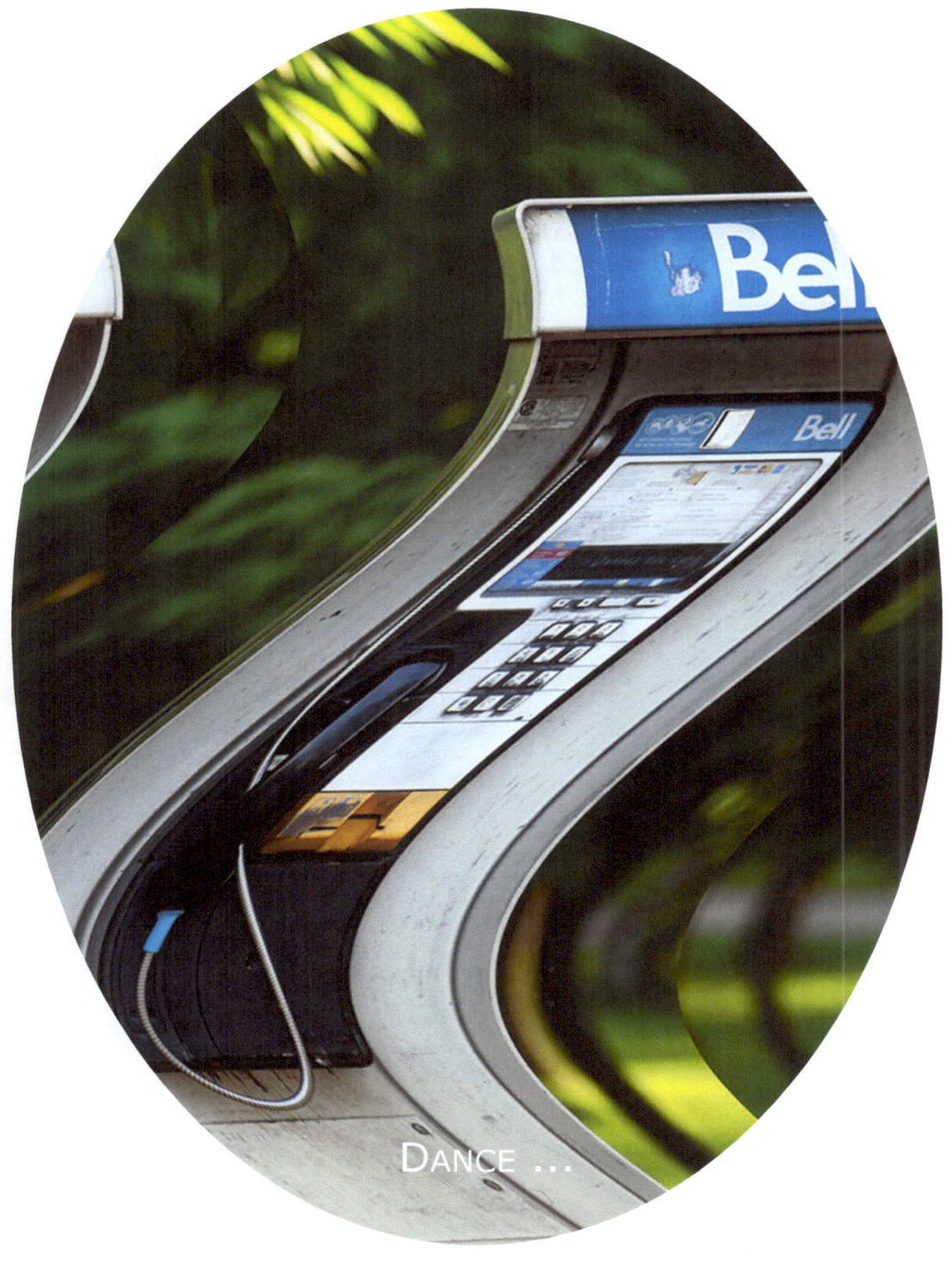

DANCE ...

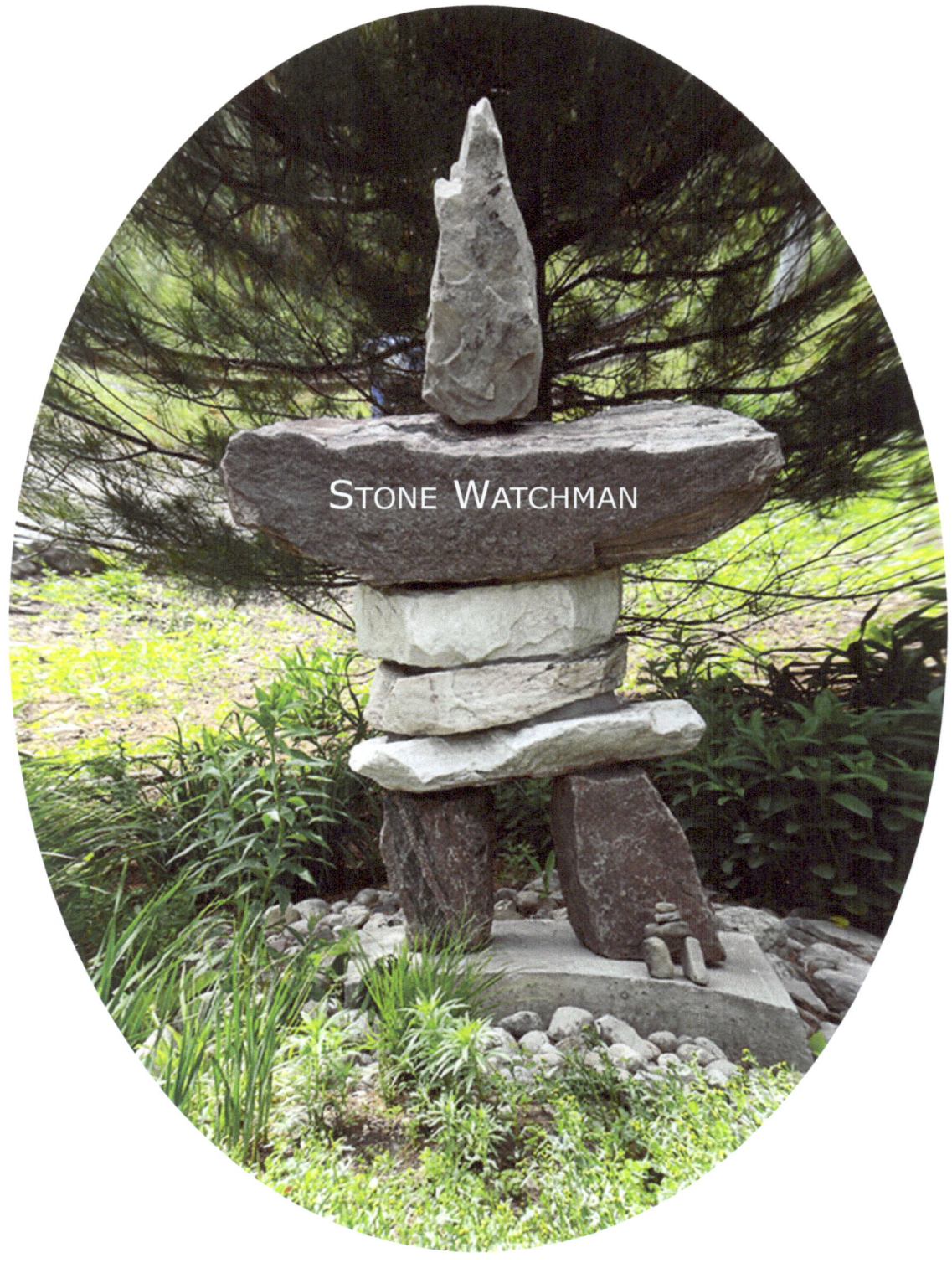

STONE WATCHMAN

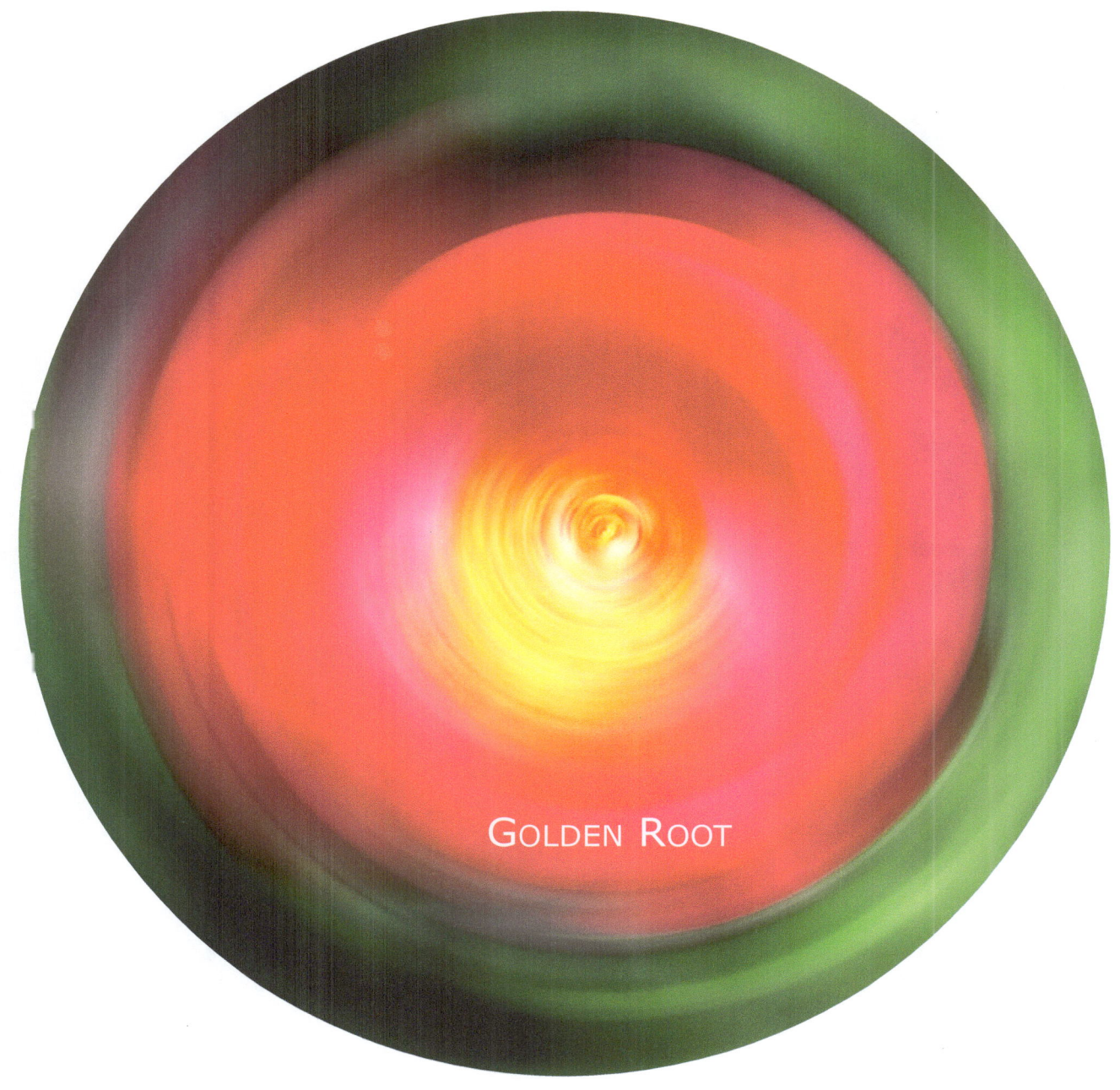

GOLDEN ROOT

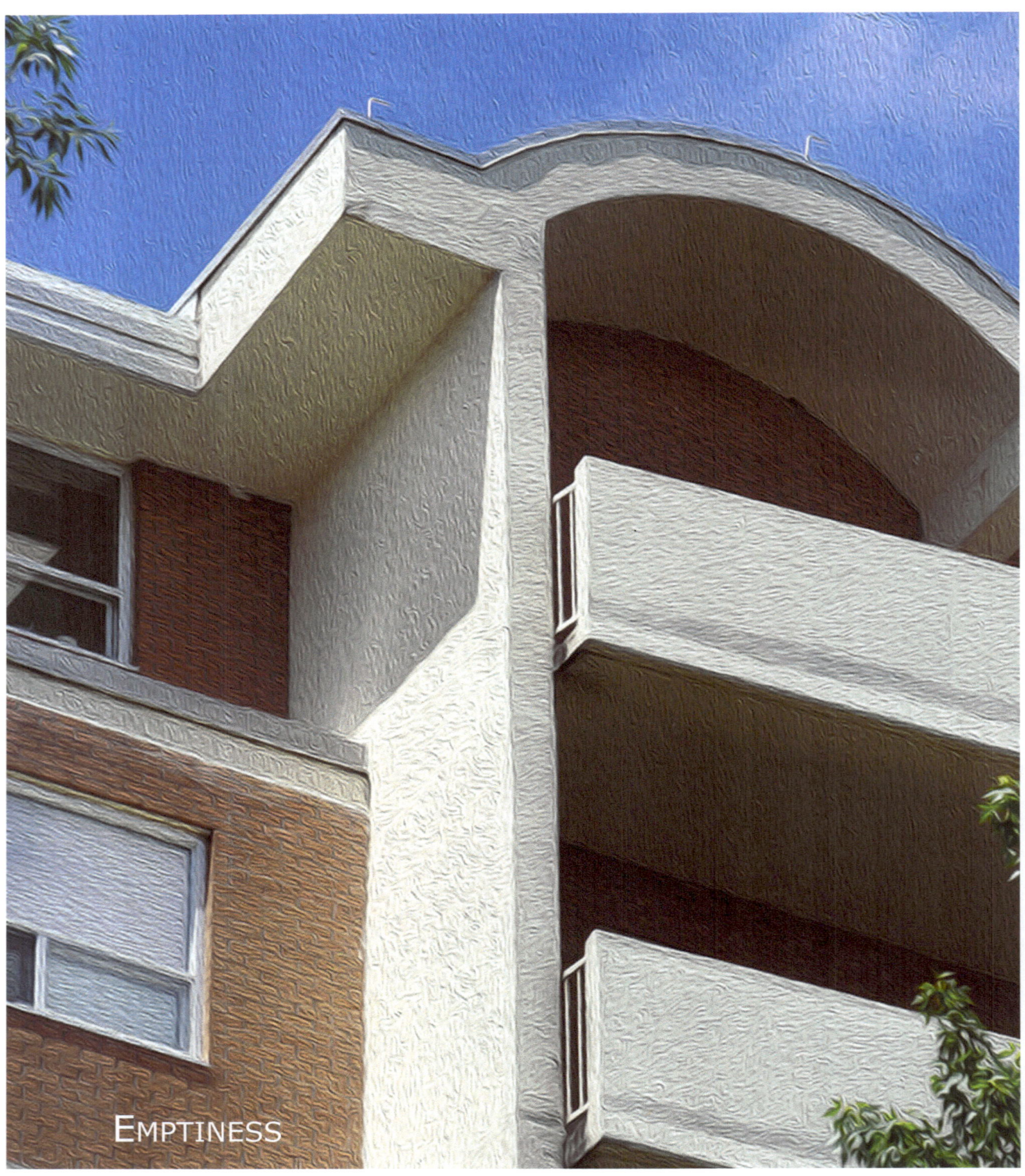

EMPTINESS

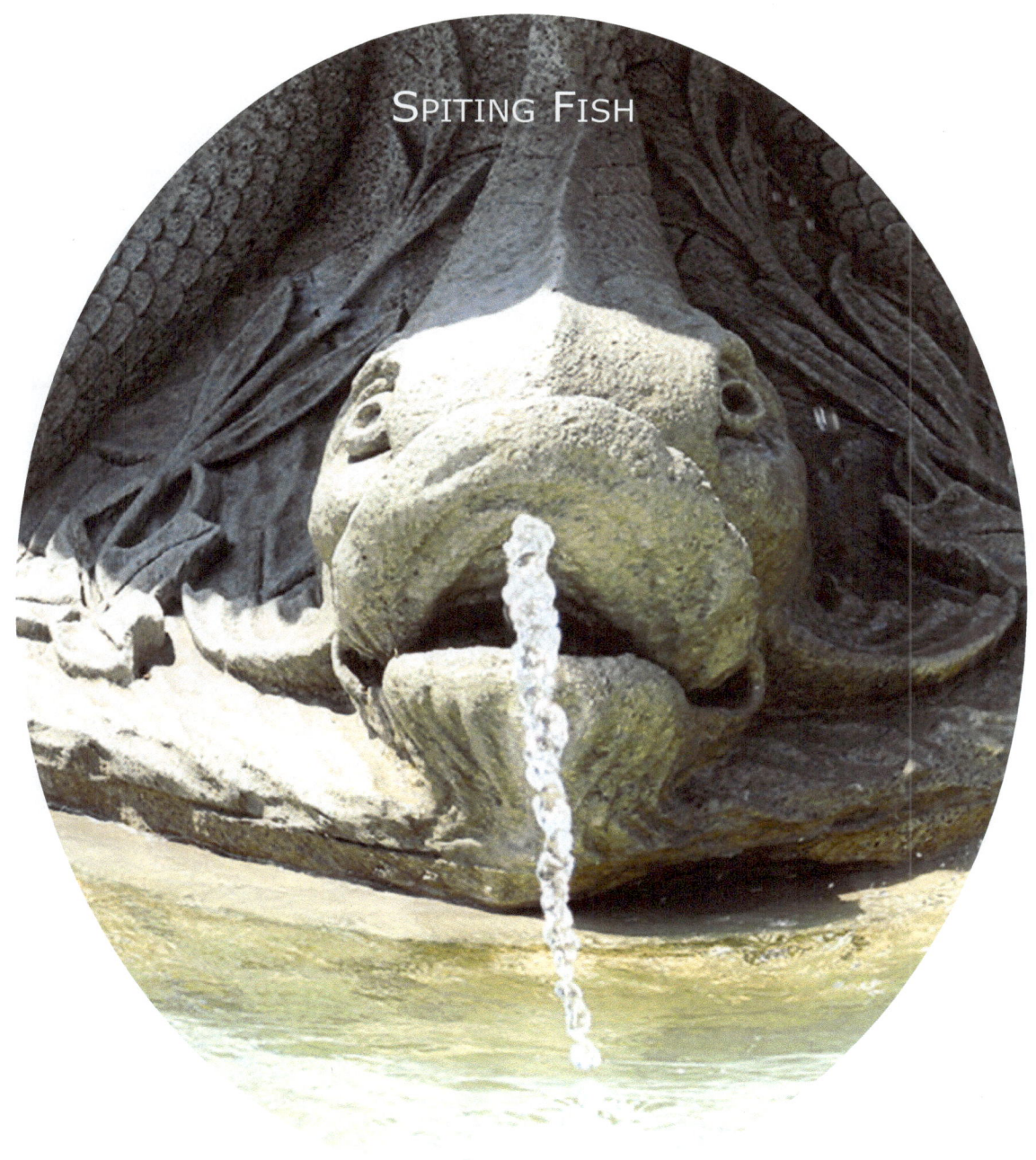

SPITING FISH

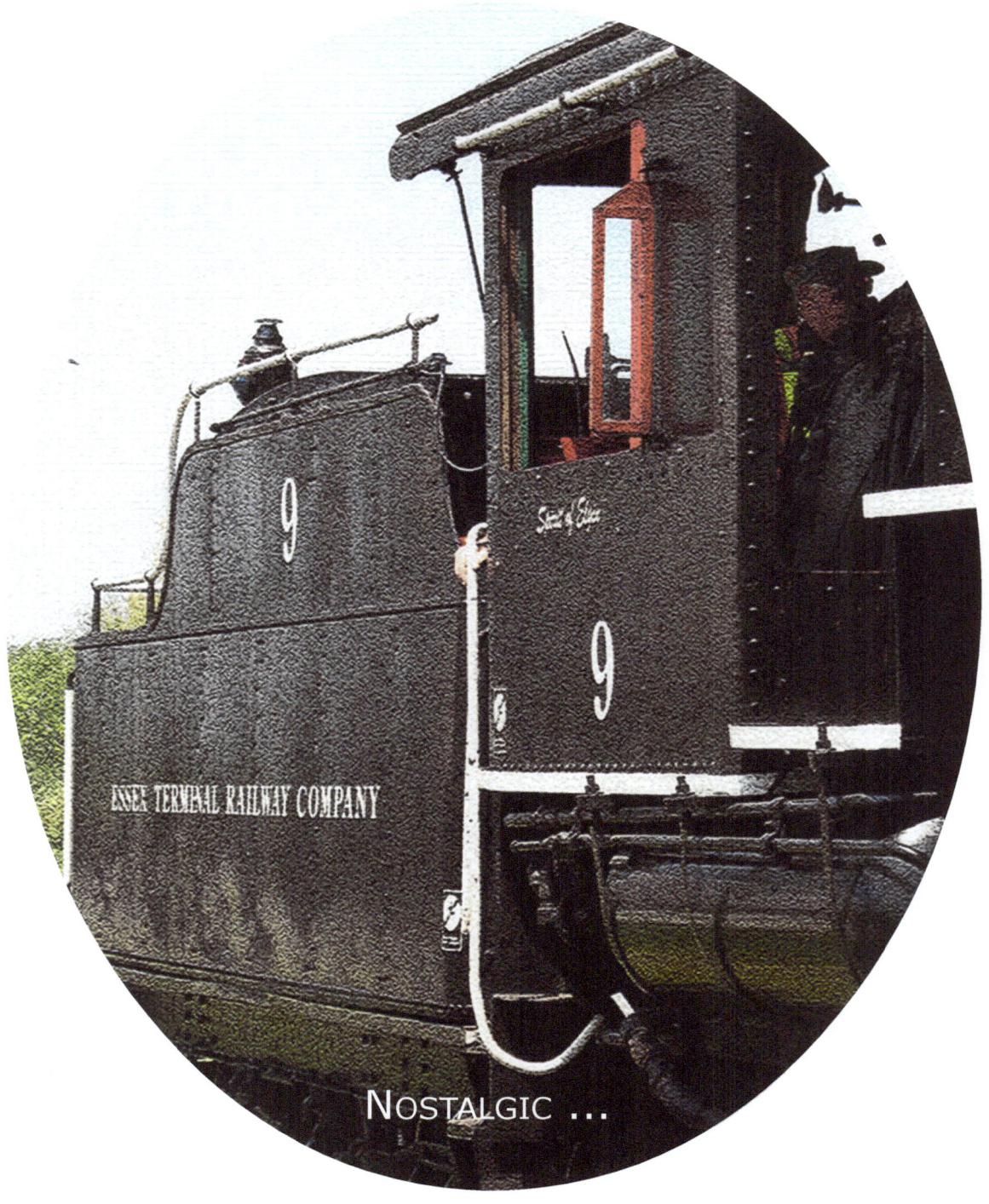

NOSTALGIC …

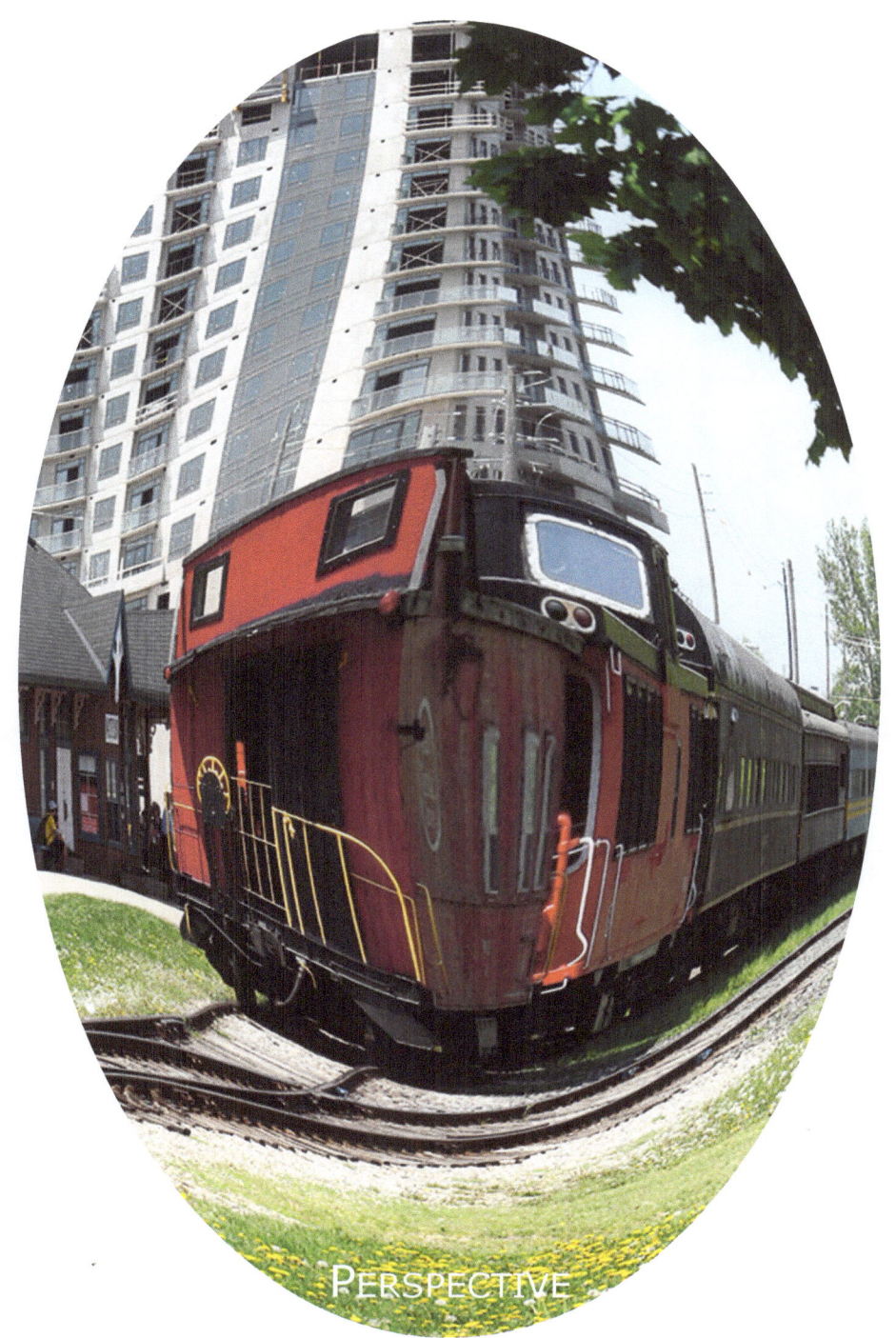

PERSPECTIVE

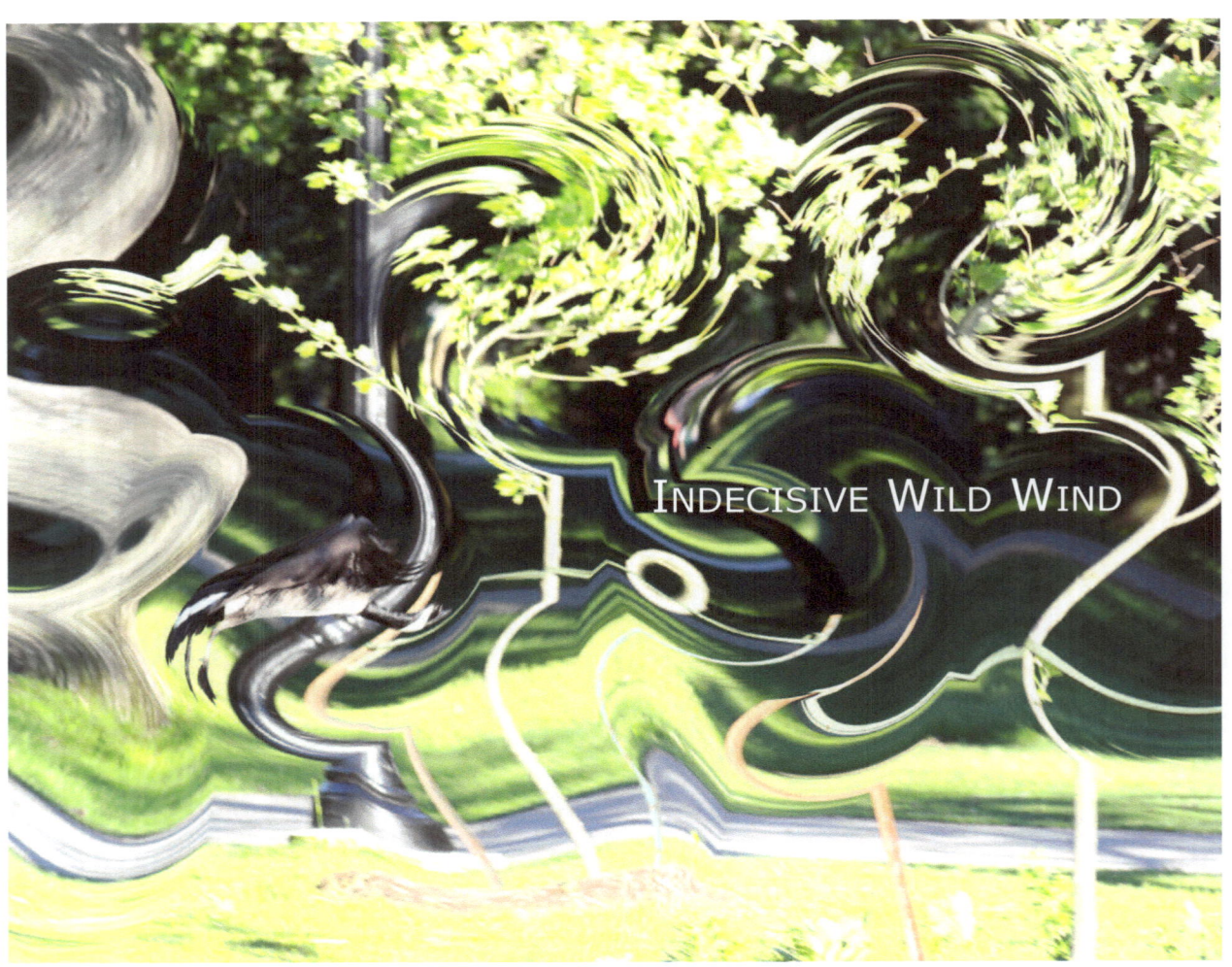

INDECISIVE WILD WIND

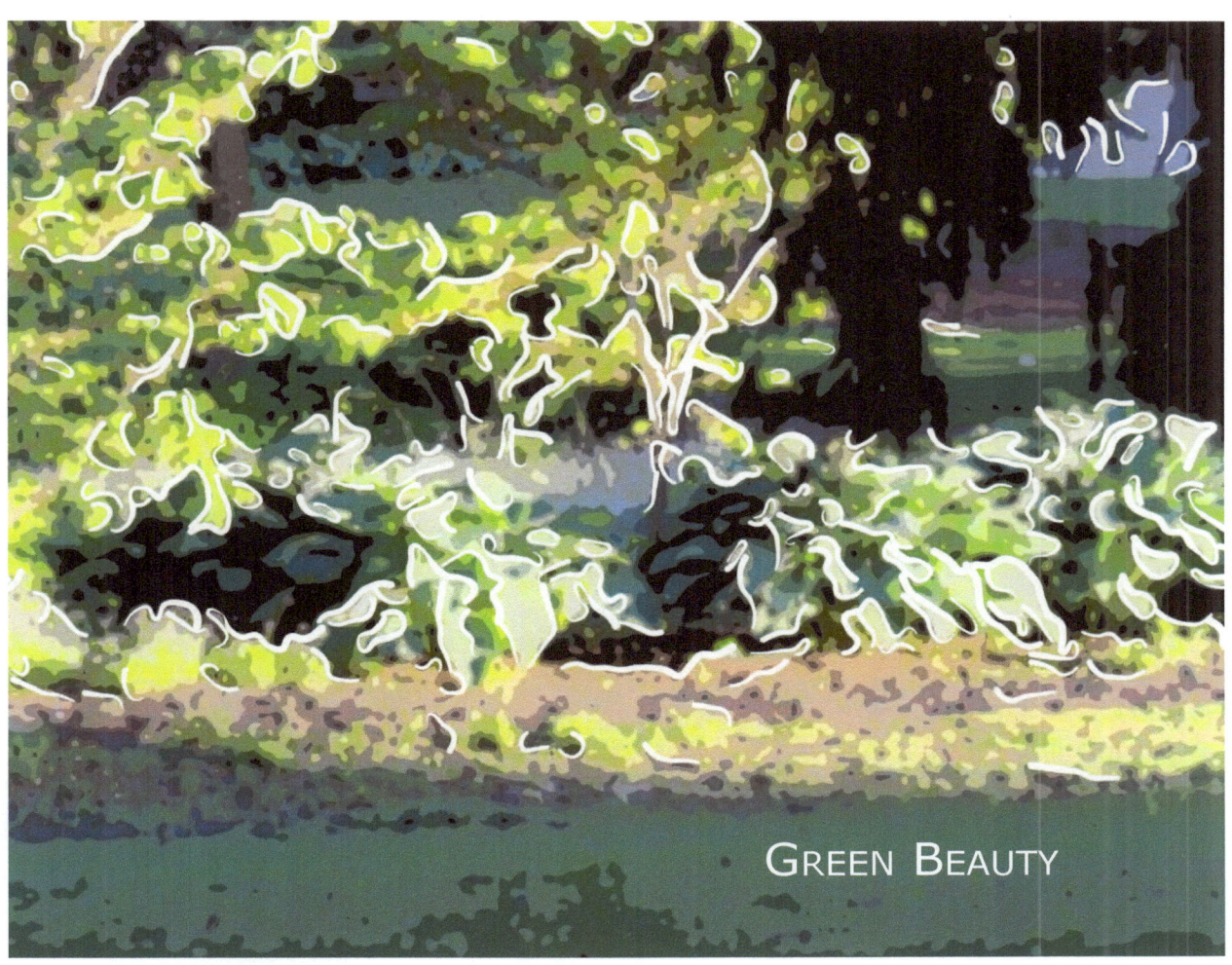

GREEN BEAUTY

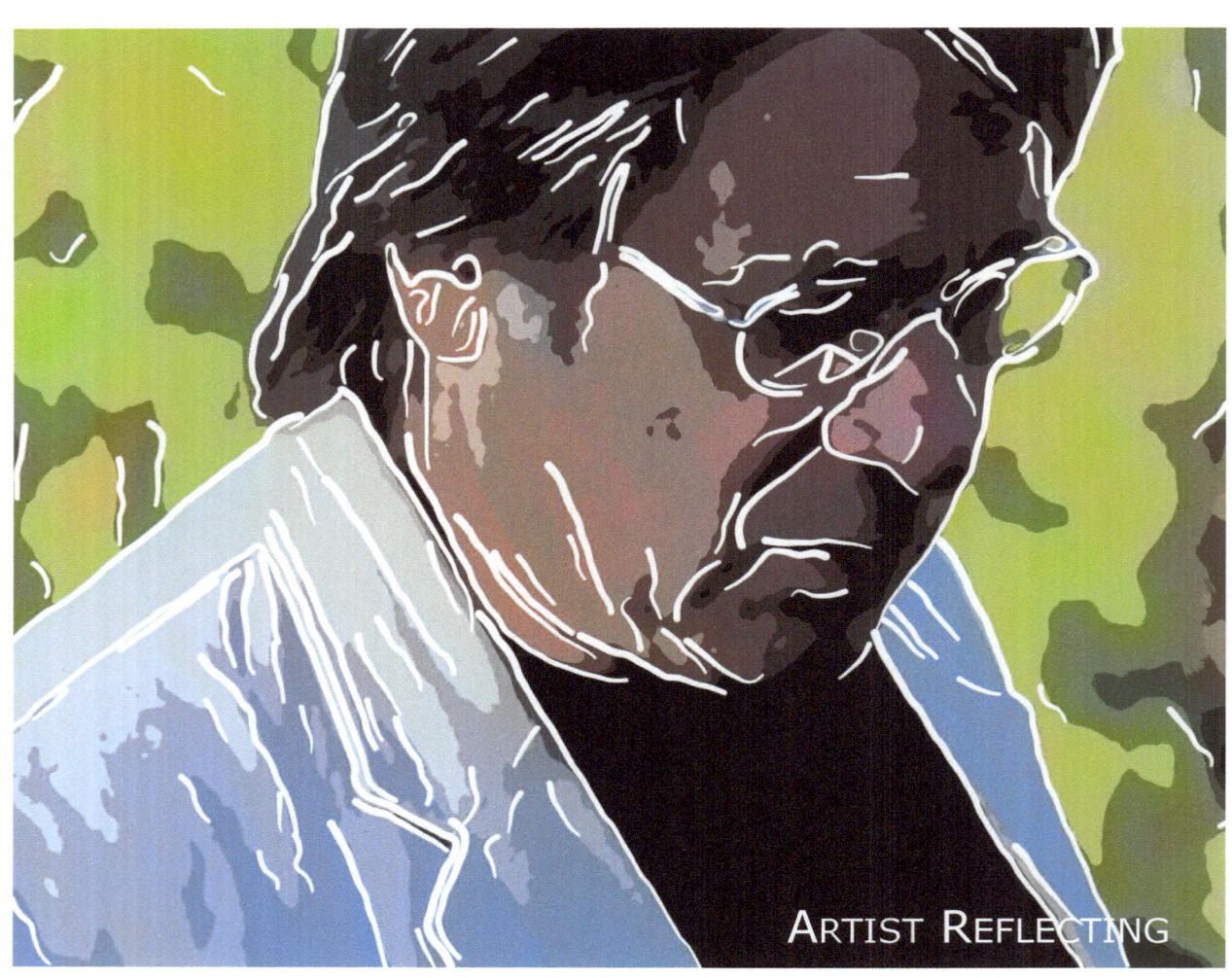

ARTIST REFLECTING

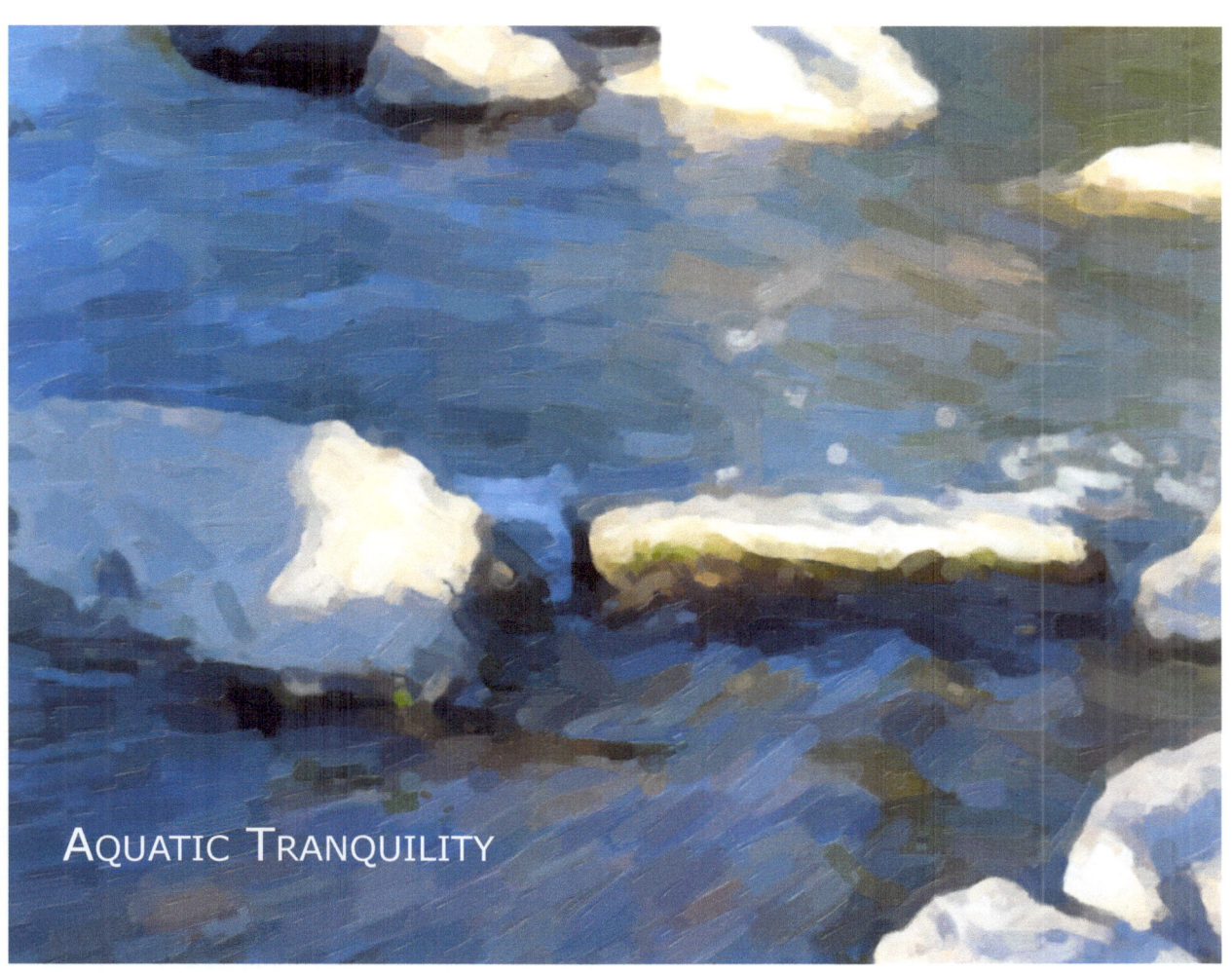

AQUATIC TRANQUILITY

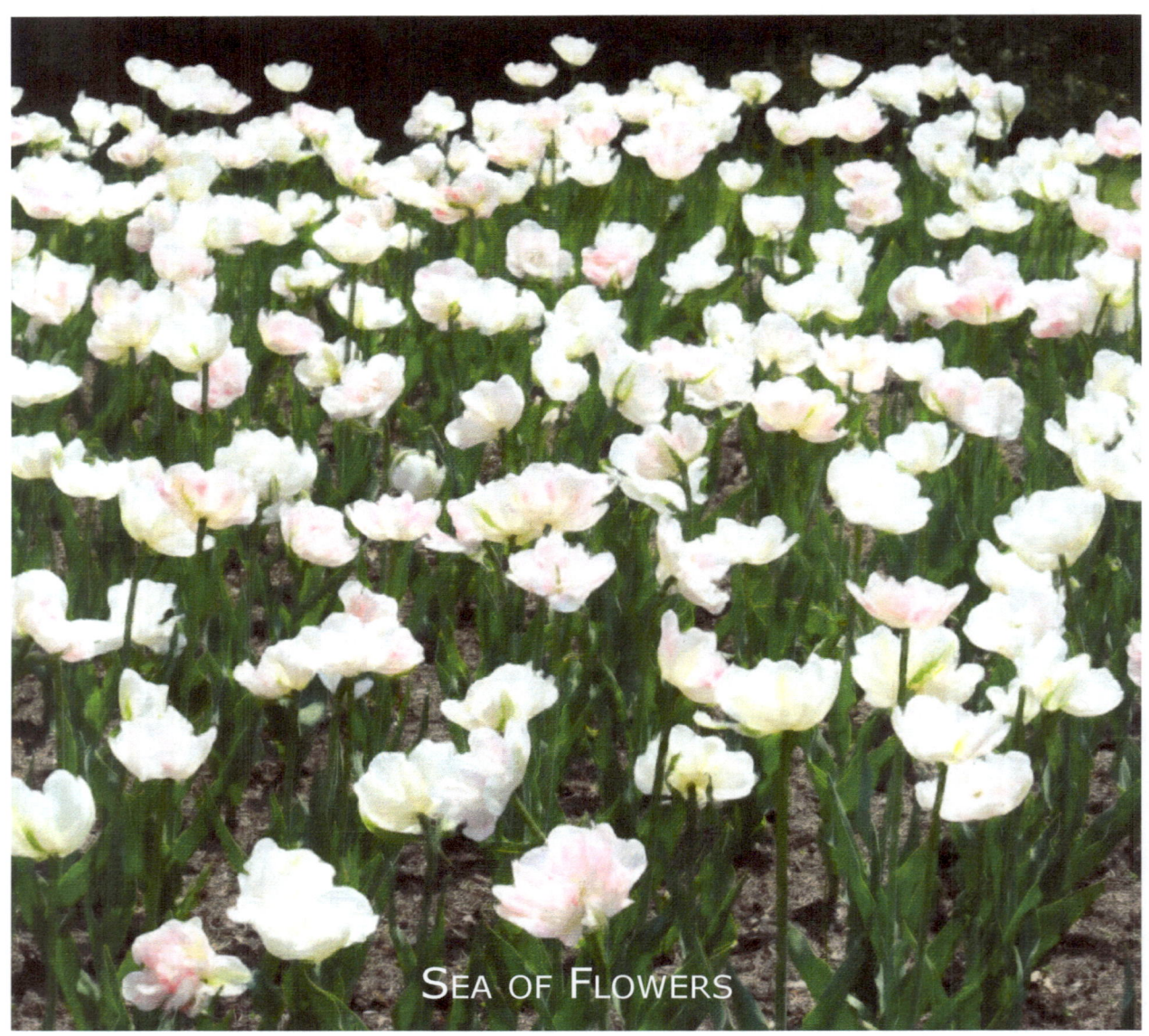

SEA OF FLOWERS

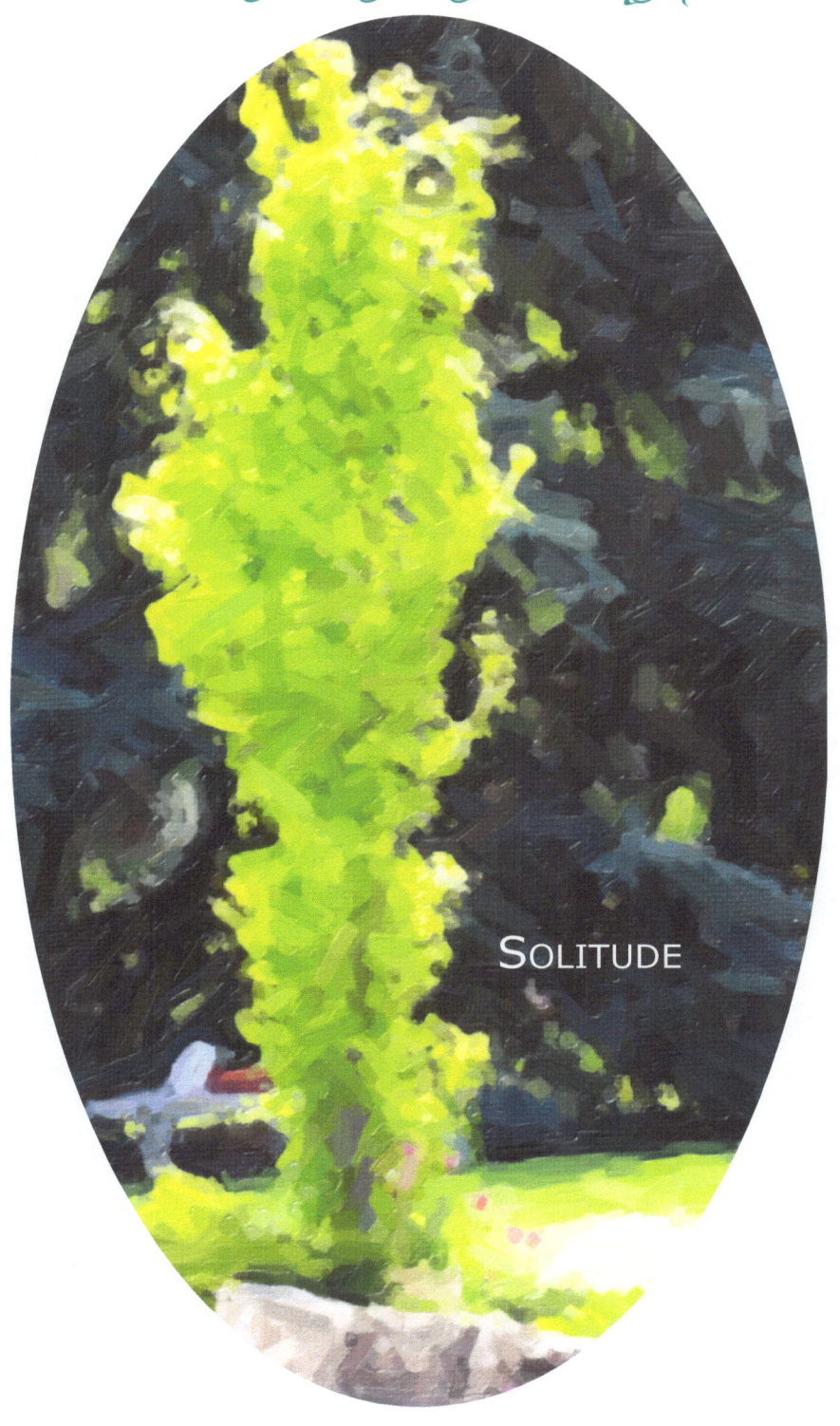

SOLITUDE

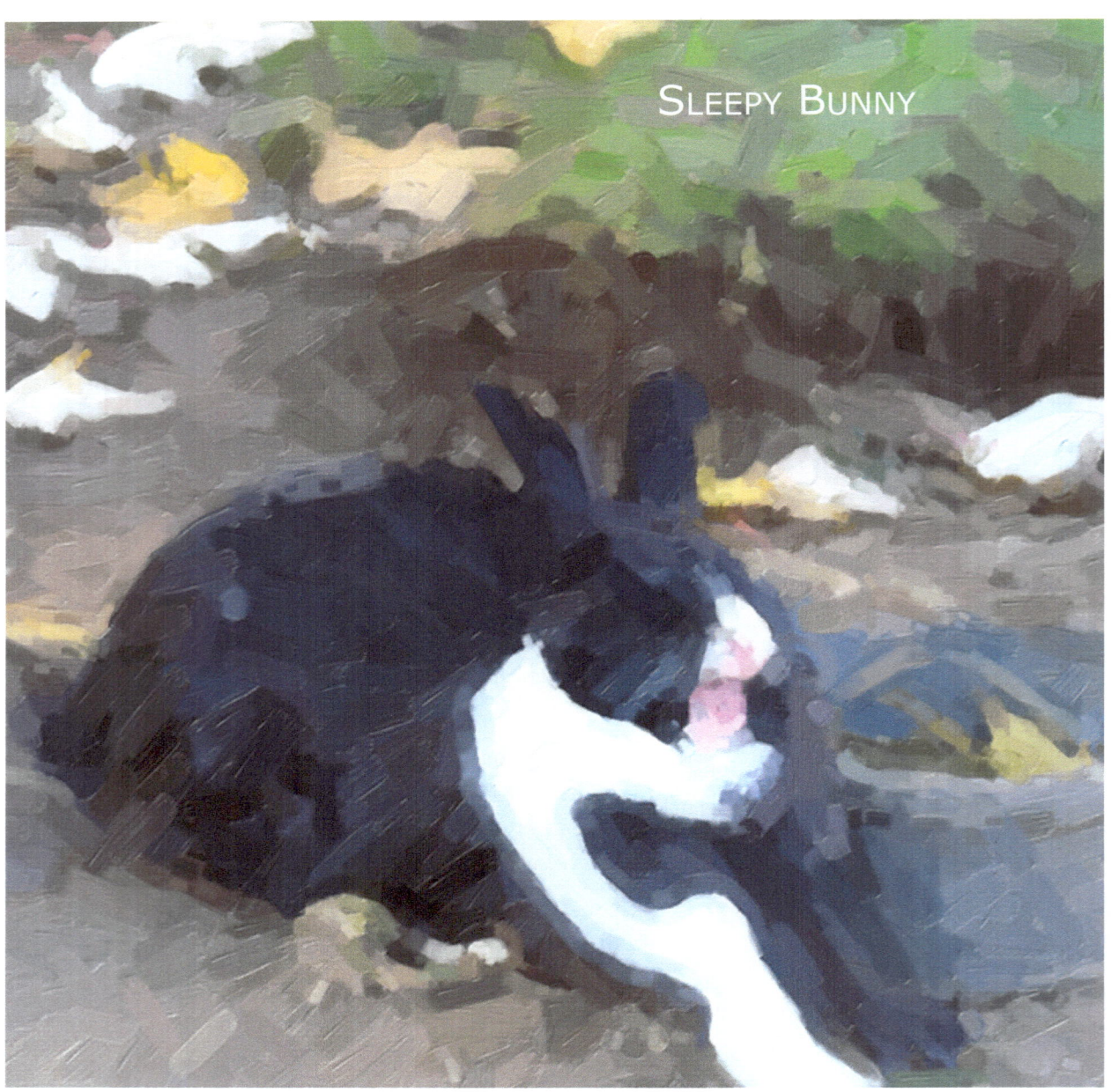

SLEEPY BUNNY

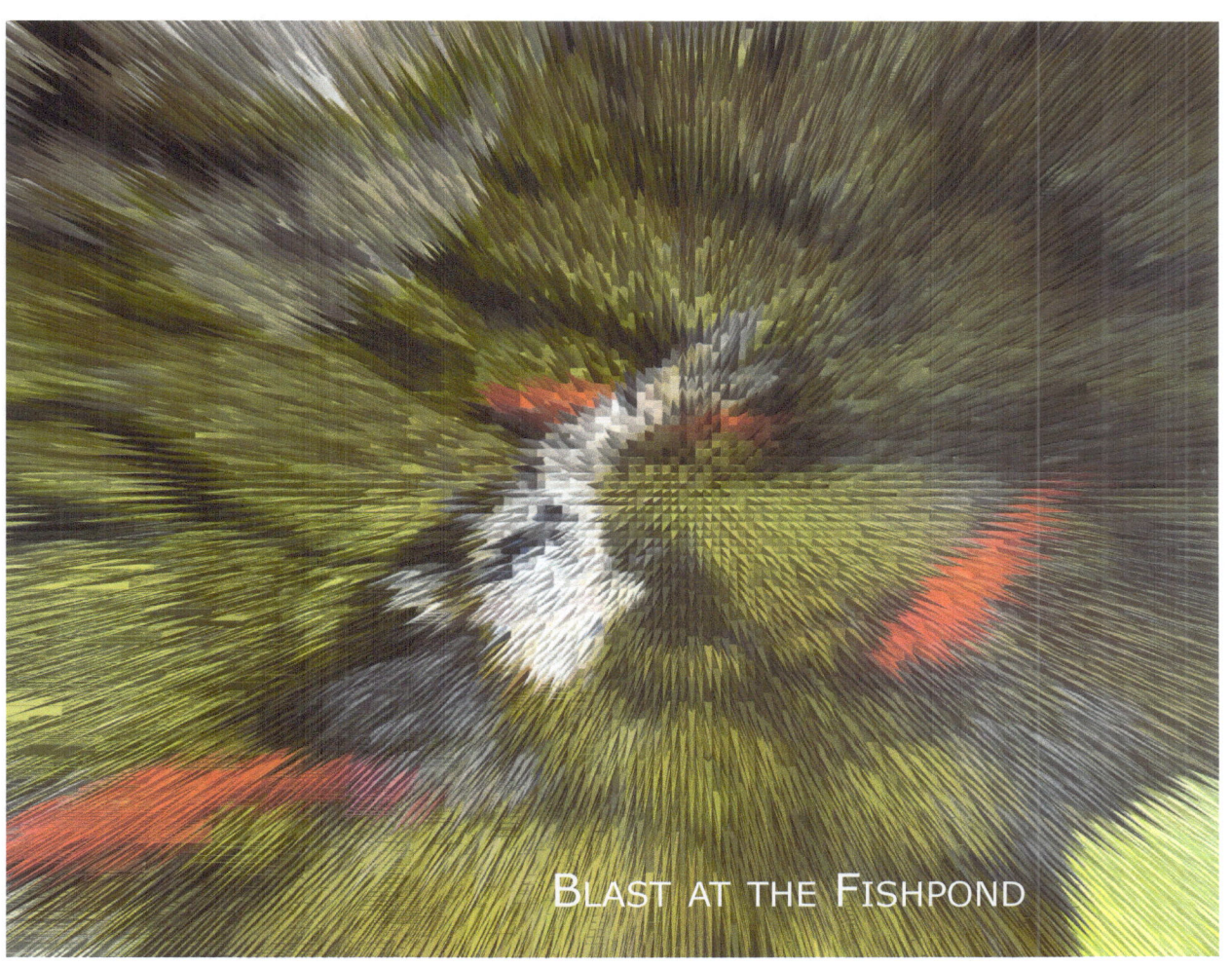

BLAST AT THE FISHPOND

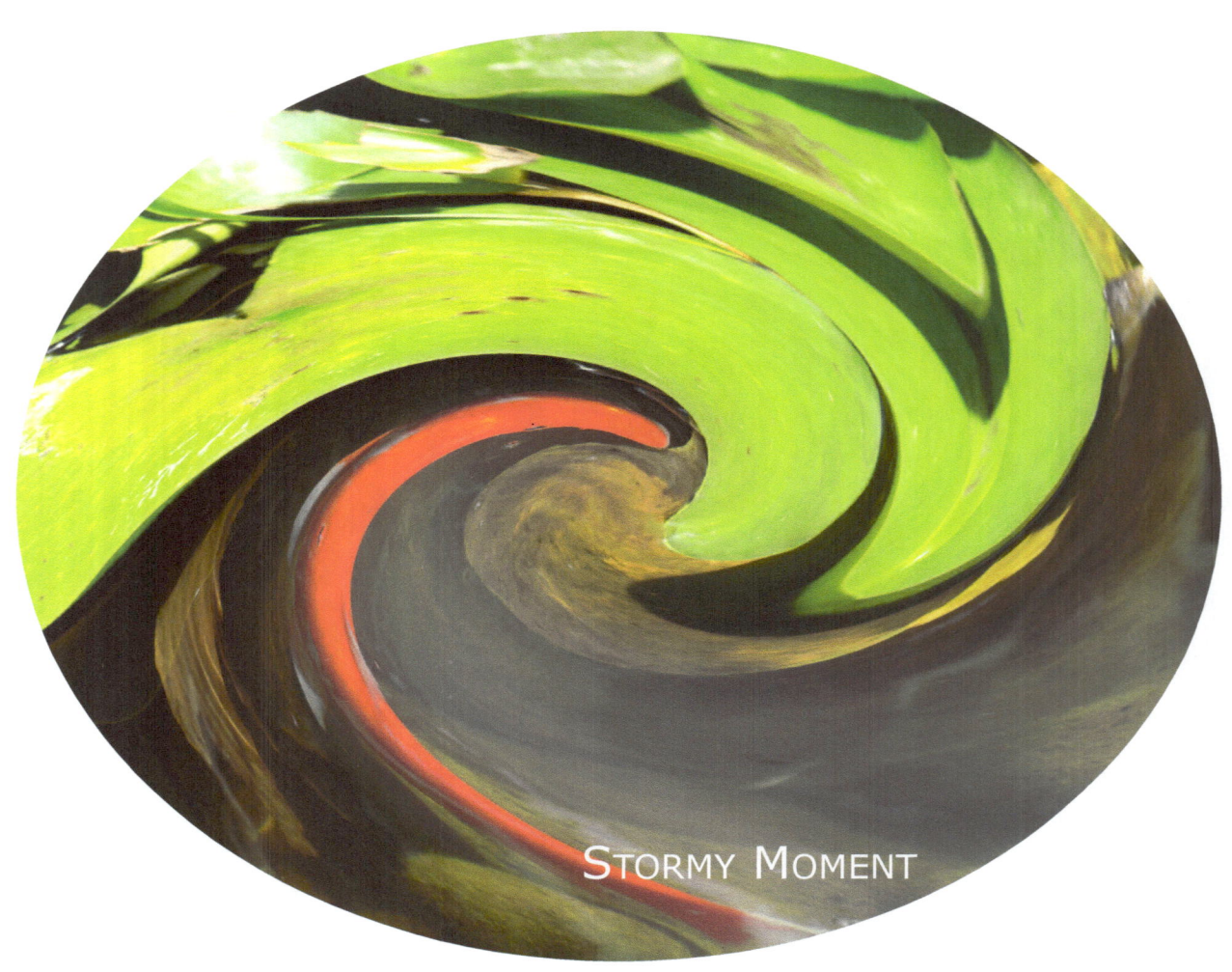

STORMY MOMENT

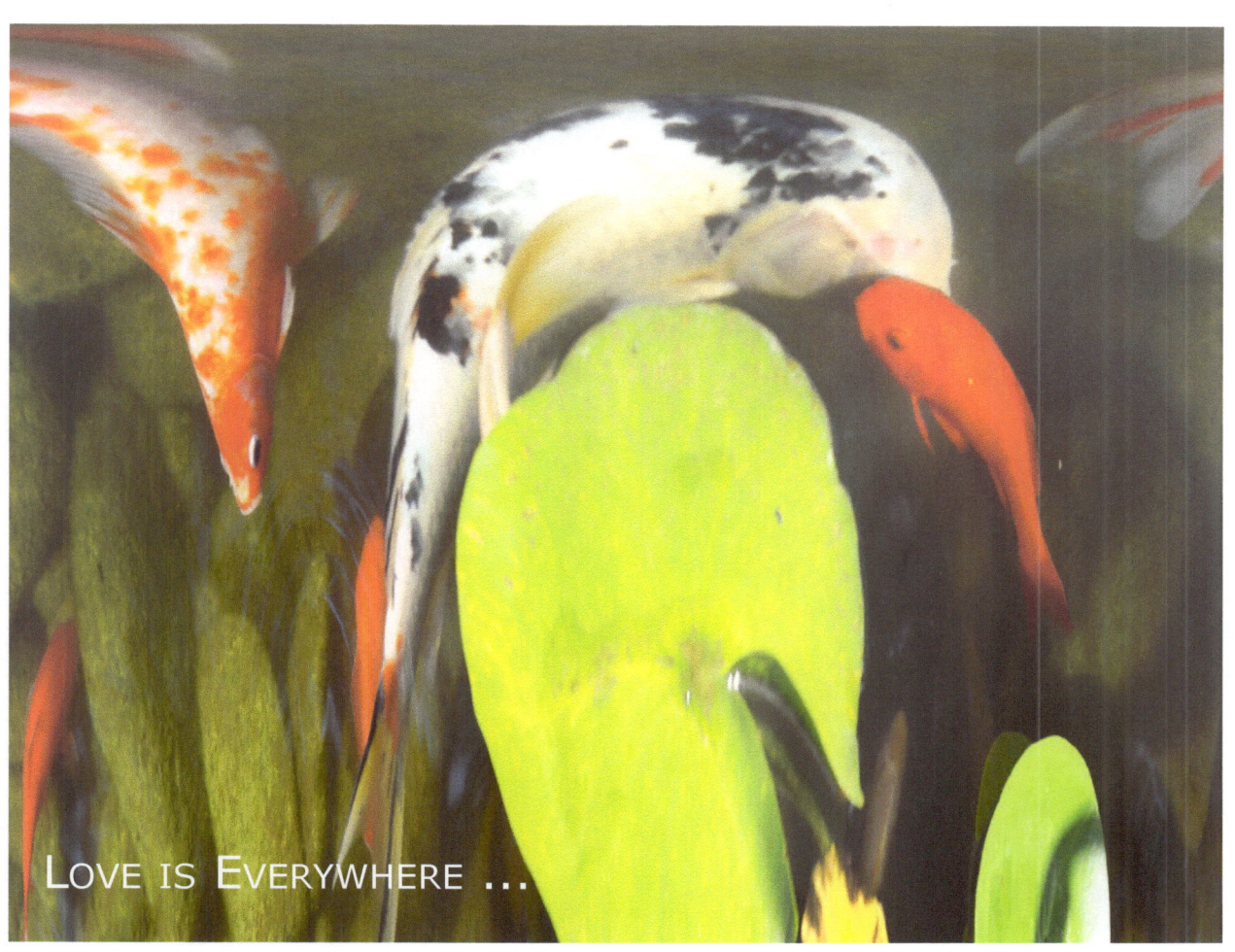

LOVE IS EVERYWHERE ...

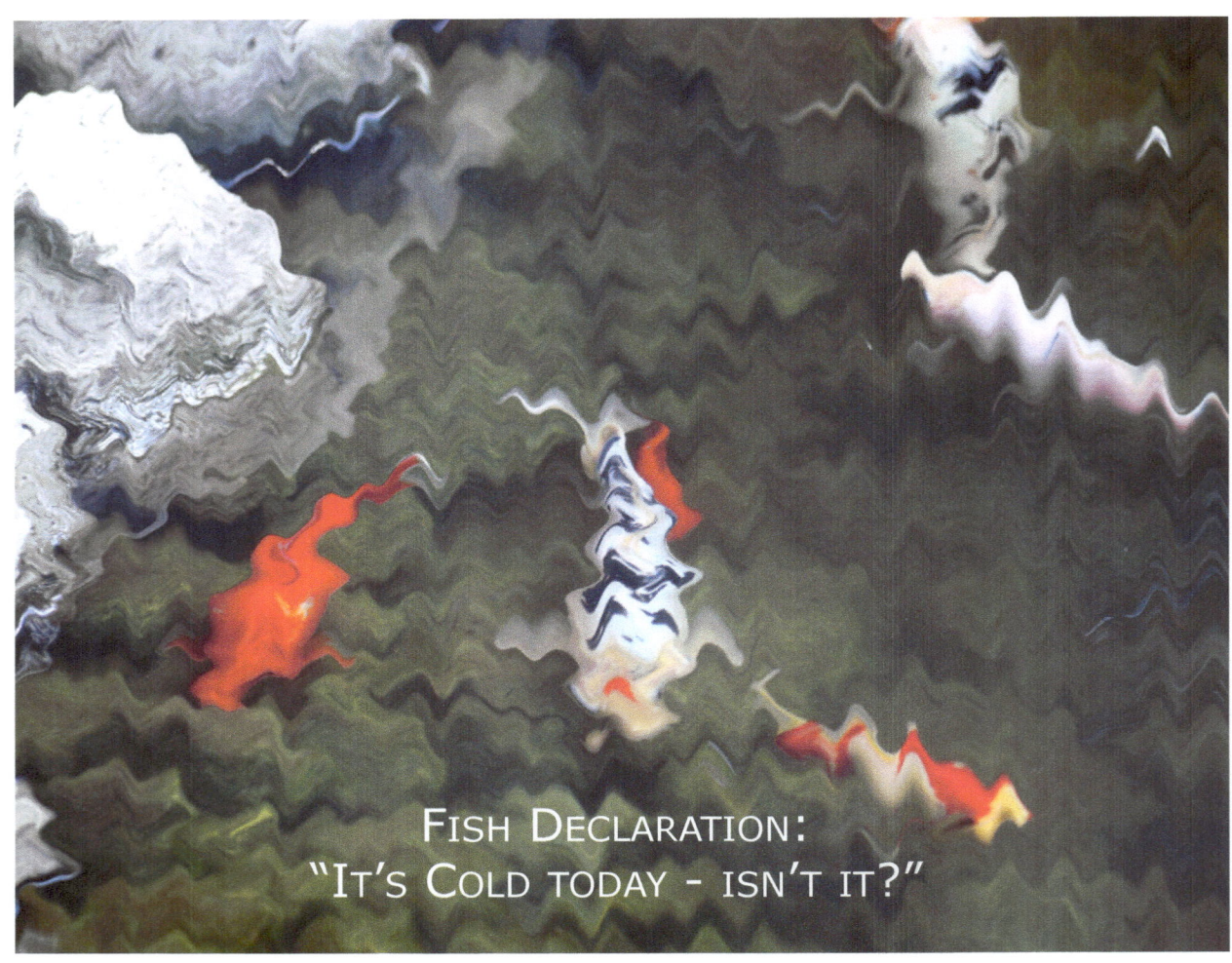

FISH DECLARATION:
"IT'S COLD TODAY - ISN'T IT?"

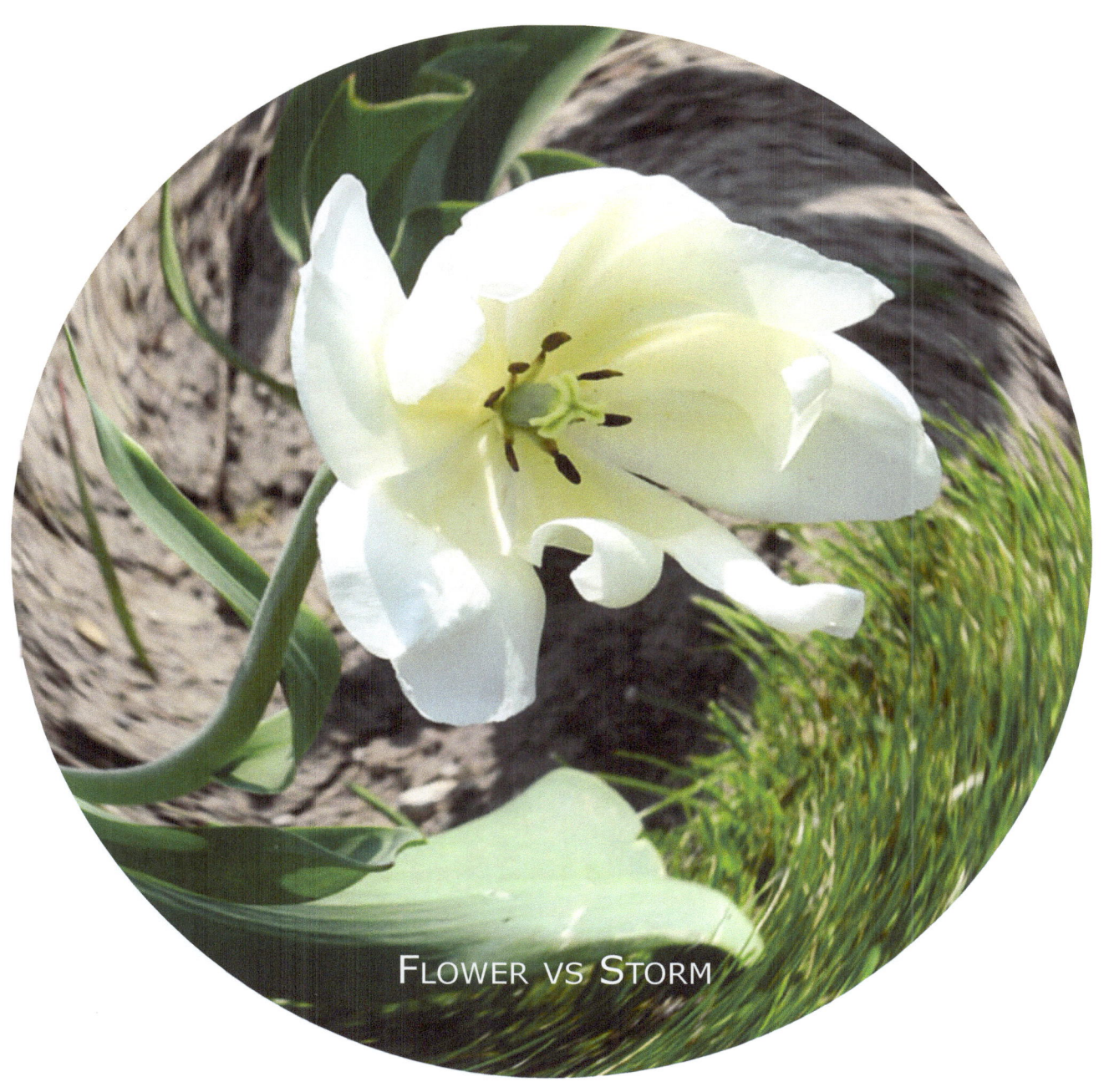

FLOWER VS STORM

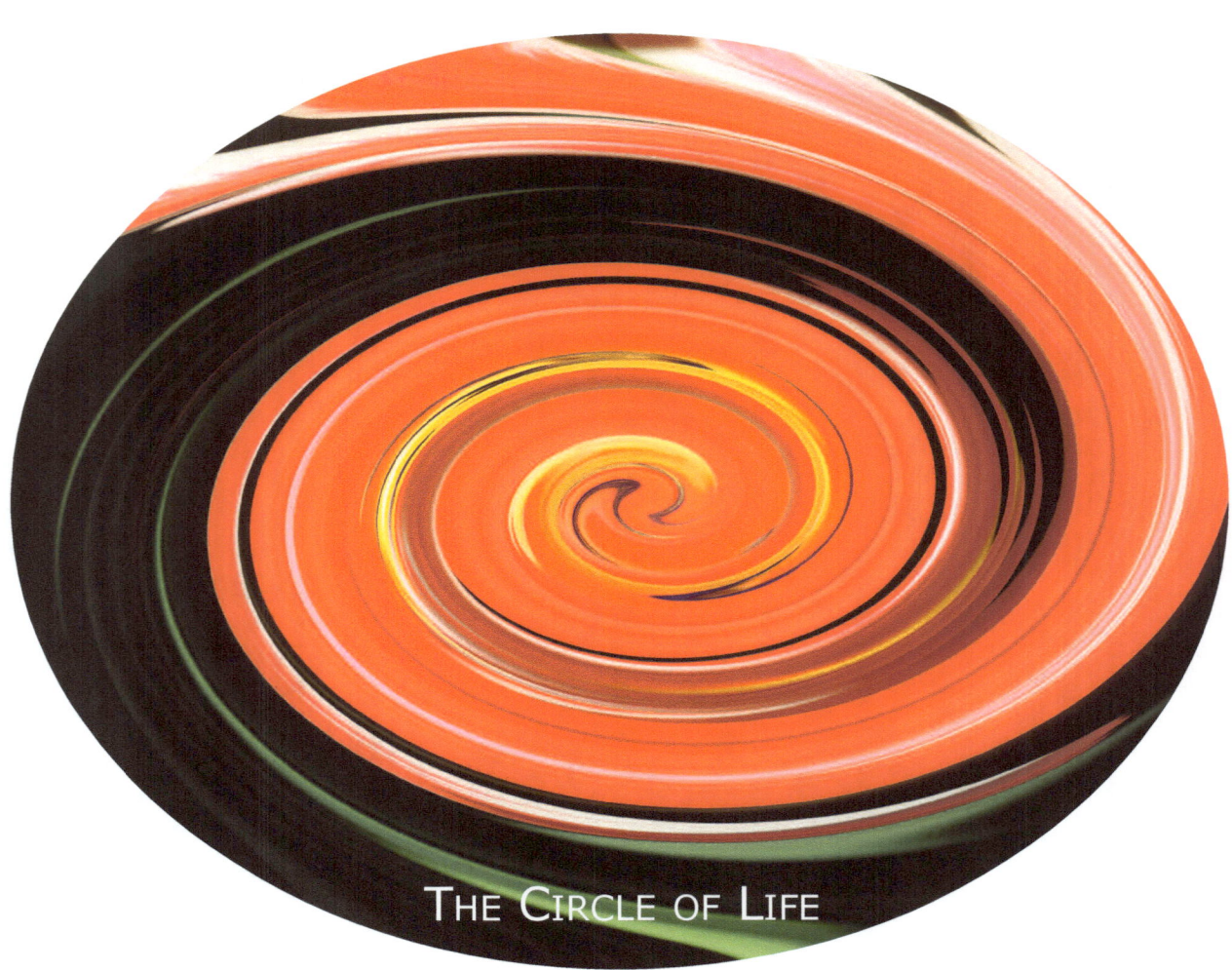

THE CIRCLE OF LIFE

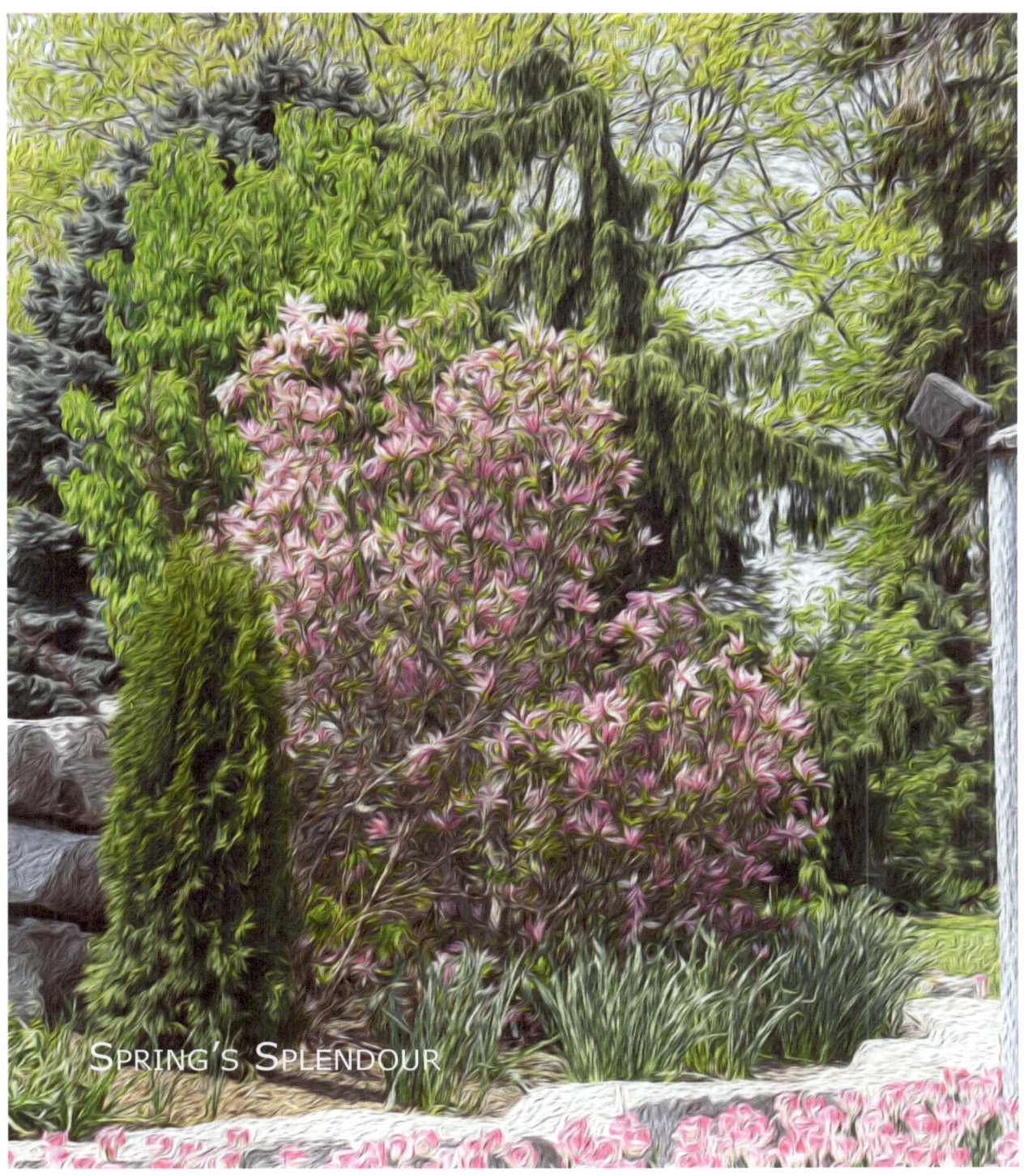

SPRING'S SPLENDOUR

BIBLIOGRAPHY—KLAUS D. EMRICH

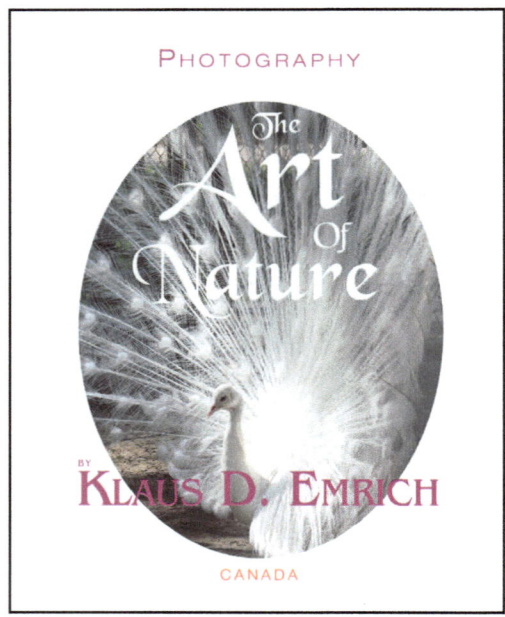

BOOKS ALSO AVAILABLE IN GERMAN LANGUAGE.

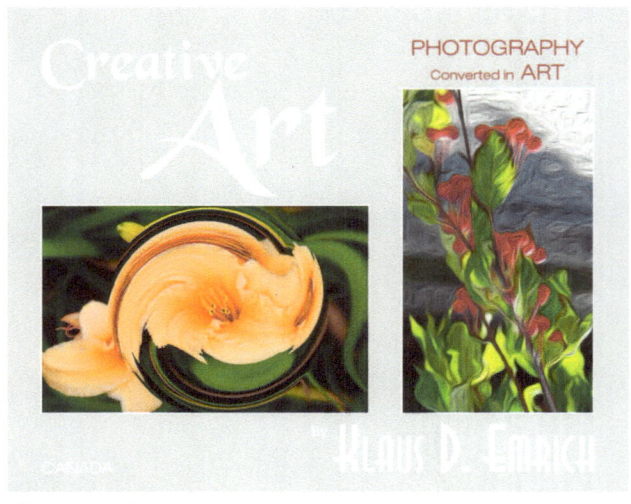

THE ART OF NATURE
Photography - Canadian nature.

CREATIVE ART
Artistic view via photography.

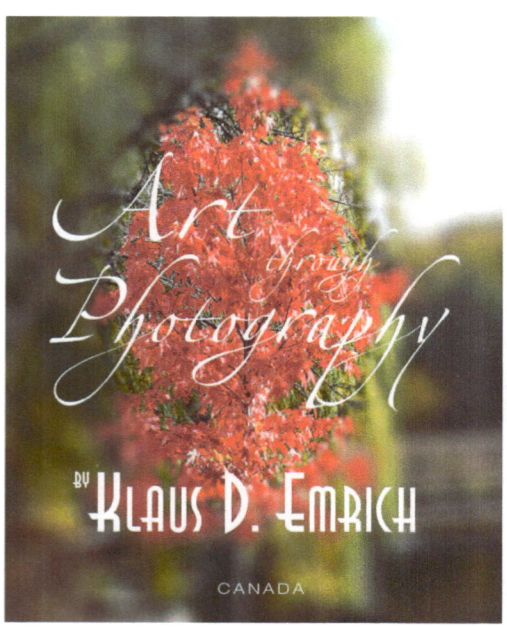

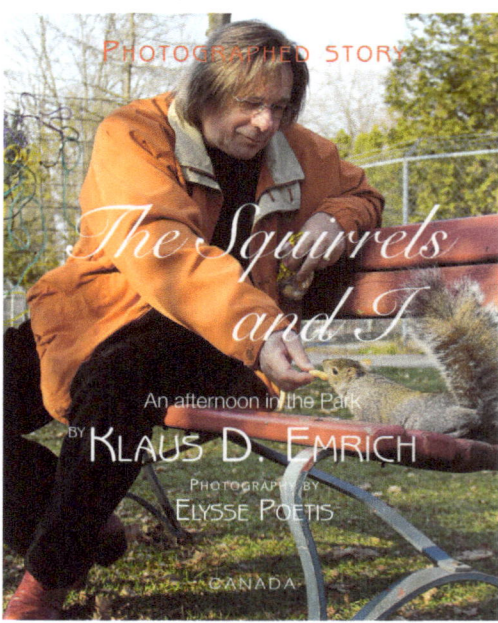

ART THROUGH PHOTOGRAPHY
Photography converted into art.

THE SQUIRRELS AND I
Photographed story.

ABOUT THE AUTHOR

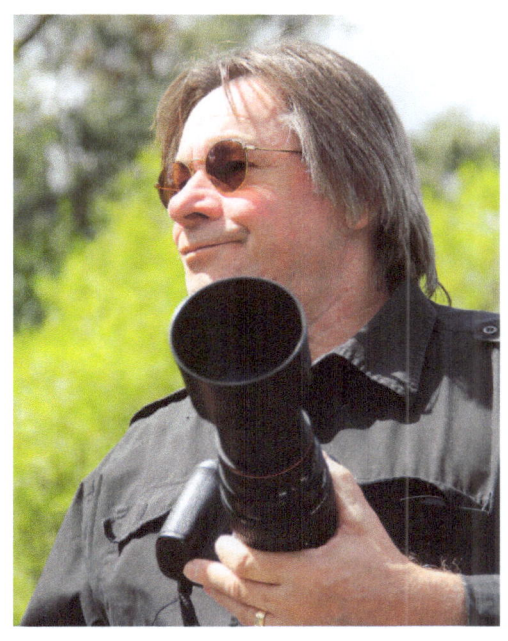

Klaus D. Emrich loved to create art since he was a small child back in Germany. He would explore nature's fields and just stare at its beauty. Only in recent years did Klaus D. started using his talent/imagination via photography. Creating beauty was always his greatest dream. "Art through Photography" was published in April 2014 by Von Der Alps Publishing Corporation. Klaus D. is the author of multiple books, with many more to come.

Klaus D. Emrich and his wife Mary Emrich, (pseudonym Elysse Poetis, Award Winning author of many books on Amazon), reside in the famous Region of Waterloo, Ontario, CANADA.

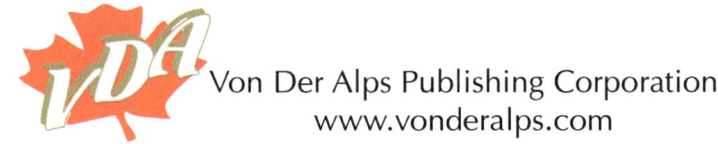 Von Der Alps Publishing Corporation
www.vonderalps.com